Mel Bay's Best Scale Method for Any Instrument

by Collin Bay

1 2

Visit us on the Web at www.melbay.com — E-mail us at email@melbay.com

Table of Contents

Introduction

I'm going to be perfectly honest with you: there aren't very many things I enjoy doing less than practicing scales. Still, if I practice only one thing, it almost always ends up being scales. They simply are of prime importance. There are tons of reasons to practice scales—scales may not be musical, but they give you the tactile knowledge of your instrument and facility necessary to fluently play any melody or musical motif thrown your way. They are great vehicles to improve your technique and velocity. They help you improve your tone. Their very nature—namely their function outside of specific repertoire—allows you to focus on the technical things you ideally relegate to your subconscious when performing music in a real-world context.

This book isn't a scale encyclopedia; rather, it provides a comprehensive way to practice scales (and for that matter, arpeggios, chords and patterns). You will be given a routine to practice full-register scales; you will be shown ways to practice connecting scales from one key with those from any other key; you will be given a way to deal with each directional movement, and any intervallic structure. This book will provide you with the most efficient way to practice scales and the fastest path to mastery of your instrument.

Part One

In this section, pick a scale or mode you'd like to practice—perhaps start with the major scale until you're familiar with this book's methodology. There are six different root movements (chromatic; whole-step; minor third; major third; perfect fourth; tritone) and four directional movements (all ascending; all descending; ascending then descending; descending then ascending). Practice these exercises using single-octave scales; then two-octave; then three, and so on. I will use the range of the guitar for all of the examples in this book, but the exercises can be adapted to fit the range of any instrument.

Chromatic ("Half-Step") Root Movement

Single-octave scales
All ascending, low to high

All ascending, high to low

All descending, low to high

All descending, high to low

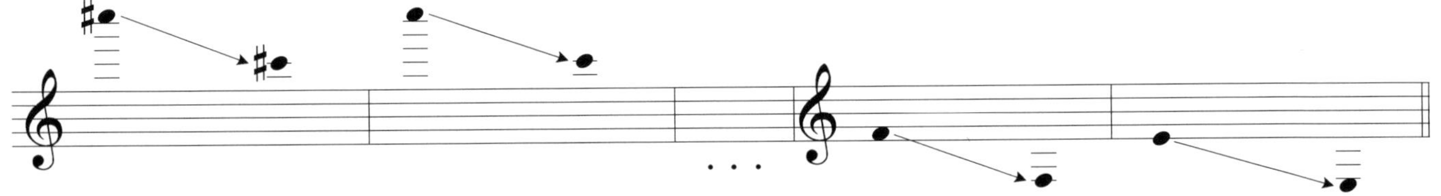

Ascending then descending, low to high

Ascending then descending, high to low

Descending then ascending, low to high

Descending then ascending, high to low

Two-octave scales

All ascending, low to high

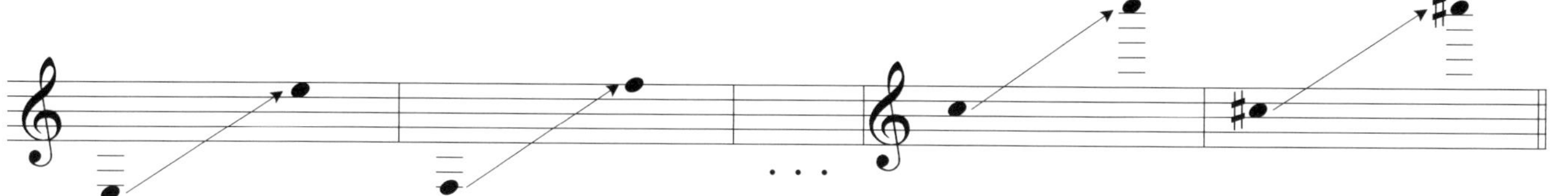

All ascending, high to low

All descending, low to high

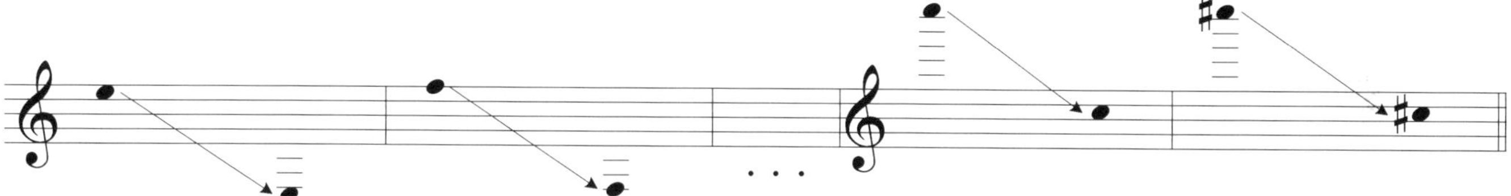

All descending, high to low

Ascending then descending, low to high

Ascending then descending, high to low

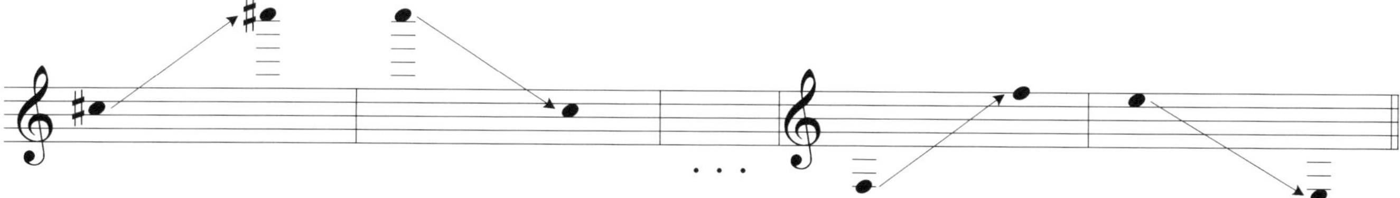

Descending then ascending, low to high

Descending then ascending, high to low

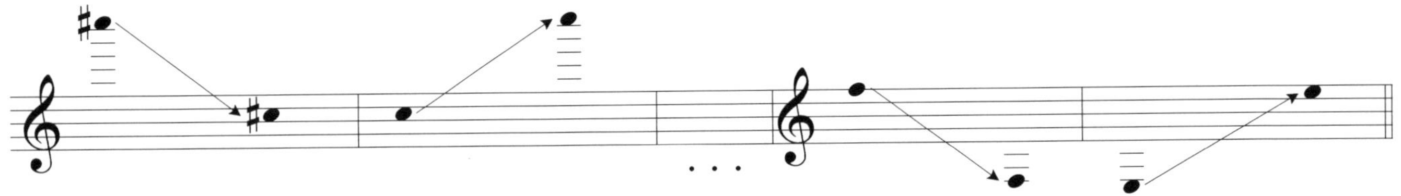

Three-octave scales
All ascending, low to high

All ascending, high to low

All descending, low to high

All descending, high to low

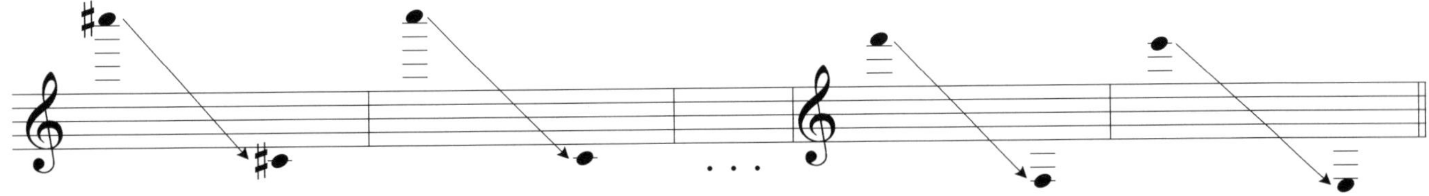

Ascending then descending, low to high

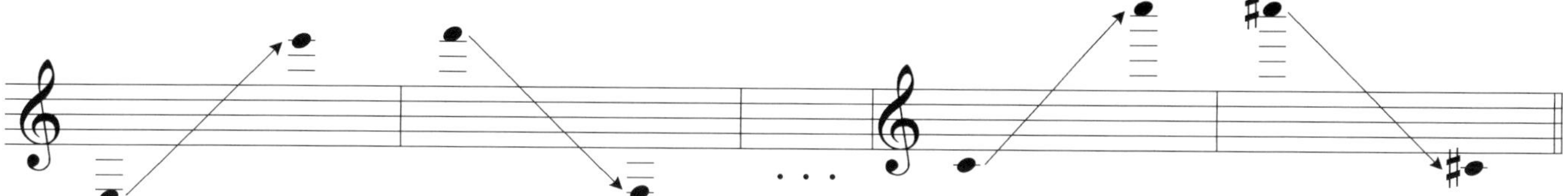

Ascending then descending, high to low

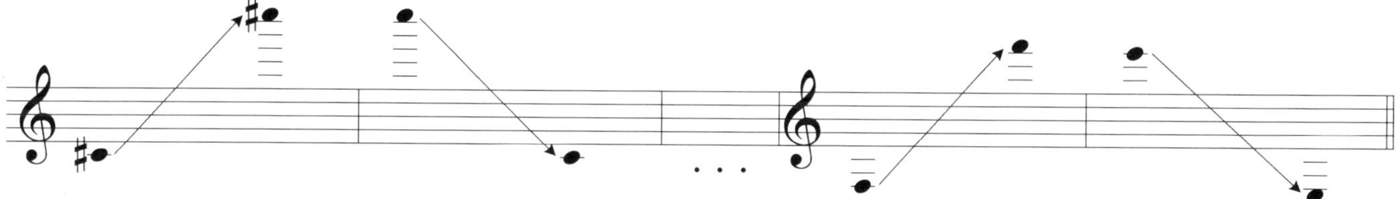

Descending then ascending, low to high

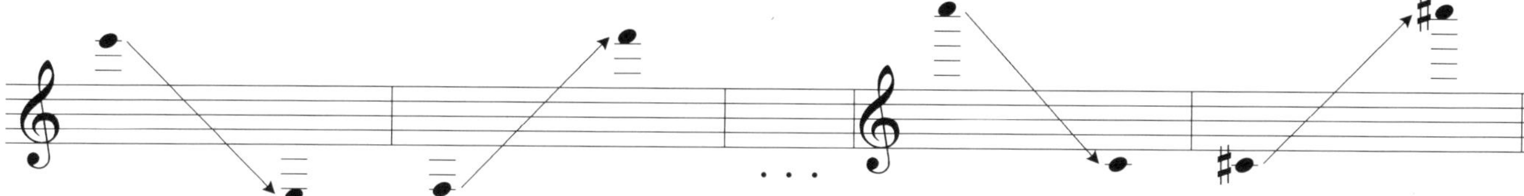

Descending then ascending, high to low

Full-range scales, lowest root to highest root

All ascending, root movement ascending (for example, E major first; then F and so on)

All descending, root movement ascending

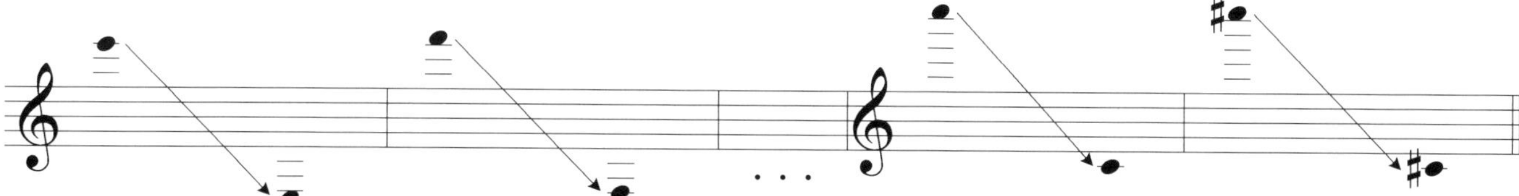

Ascending then descending, root movement ascending

Descending then ascending, root movement ascending

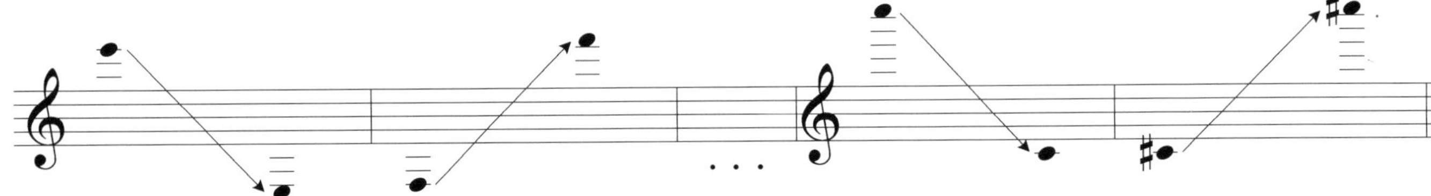

All ascending, root movement descending (E first; then F and so on)

All descending, root movement descending

Ascending then descending, root movement descending

Descending then ascending, root movement descending

Full-range scales, lowest scale tone to highest scale tone

All ascending, root movement ascending (for example, E major first; then F and so on)

All descending, root movement ascending

Ascending then descending, root movement ascending

Descending then ascending, root movement ascending

All ascending, root movement descending (E first; then F and so on)

All descending, root movement descending

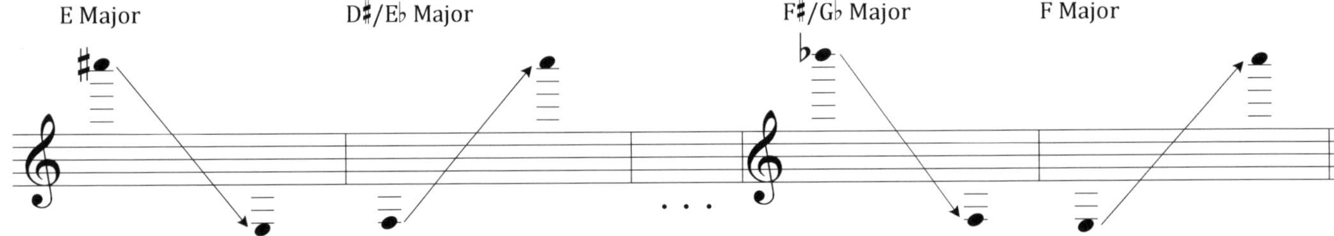

Whole-Step Root Movement

We will now go through the same exercises from the first section of the book; however, this time we will utilize whole-step root movement rather than chromatic root movement. The biggest difference between the chromatic section and this section is that you will now practice each exercise in two sets. If, for example, you are practicing single-octave scales ascending in whole steps, your root movement could look something like this: E—F♯/G♭—G♯/A♭—A♯/B♭—C—D; you would then need to repeat the exercise starting on F, so as to hit the six remaining keys (F—G—A—B—C♯/D♭—D♯/E♭). So you don't have to flip back to the first section, here are the exercises again:

Single-octave scales
    i.   All ascending, low to high
    ii.   All ascending, high to low
    iii. All descending, low to high
    iv. All descending, high to low
    v.   Ascending then descending, low to high
    vi. Ascending then descending, high to low
    vii. Descending then ascending, low to high
    viii. Descending then ascending, high to low

Two-octave scales
    i.   All ascending, low to high
    ii.   All ascending, high to low
    iii. All descending, low to high
    iv. All descending, high to low
    v.   Ascending then descending, low to high
    vi. Ascending then descending, high to low
    vii. Descending then ascending, low to high
    viii. Descending then ascending, high to low

Three-octave scales
    i.   All ascending, low to high
    ii.   All ascending, high to low
    iii. All descending, low to high
    iv. All descending, high to low

v. Ascending then descending, low to high
vi. Ascending then descending, high to low
vii. Descending then ascending, low to high
viii. Descending then ascending, high to low

Full-range scales, lowest root to highest root
i. All ascending, root movement ascending
ii. All descending, root movement ascending
iii. Ascending then descending, root movement ascending
iv. Descending then ascending, root movement ascending
v. All ascending, root movement descending
vi. All descending, root movement descending
vii. Ascending then descending, root movement descending
viii. Descending then ascending, root movement descending

Full-range scales, lowest scale tone to highest scale tone
i. All ascending, root movement ascending
ii. All descending, root movement ascending
iii. Ascending then descending, root movement ascending
iv. Descending then ascending, root movement ascending
v. All ascending, root movement descending
vi. All descending, root movement descending
vii. Ascending then descending, root movement descending
viii. Descending then ascending, root movement descending

Minor Third Root Movement

Like the second section of the book, this section mimics the exercises from the first section. Also like the second section, you'll be doing multiple sets for each exercise. In the second section, each exercise had two sets, due to the whole-step root movement; this section has three sets per exercise, due to the minor third root movement. So if you're practicing ascending single-octave scales with minor third root movements, you'd end up with this:

Set one: E—G—A♯/B♭—C♯/D♭
Set two: F—G♯/A♭—B—D
Set three: F♯/G♭—A—C—D♯/A♭

Now, go through the same exercises, using minor third root movement:

Single-octave scales
i. All ascending, low to high
ii. All ascending, high to low
iii. All descending, low to high
iv. All descending, high to low
v. Ascending then descending, low to high
vi. Ascending then descending, high to low
vii. Descending then ascending, low to high
viii. Descending then ascending, high to low

Two-octave scales
i. All ascending, low to high
ii. All ascending, high to low
iii. All descending, low to high

    iv.   All descending, high to low
    v.   Ascending then descending, low to high
    vi.   Ascending then descending, high to low
    vii.   Descending then ascending, low to high
    viii.   Descending then ascending, high to low

Three-octave scales

    i.   All ascending, low to high
    ii.   All ascending, high to low
    iii.   All descending, low to high
    iv.   All descending, high to low
    v.   Ascending then descending, low to high
    vi.   Ascending then descending, high to low
    vii.   Descending then ascending, low to high
    viii.   Descending then ascending, high to low

Full-range scales, lowest root to highest root

    i.   All ascending, root movement ascending
    ii.   All descending, root movement ascending
    iii.   Ascending then descending, root movement ascending
    iv.   Descending then ascending, root movement ascending
    v.   All ascending, root movement descending
    vi.   All descending, root movement descending
    vii.   Ascending then descending, root movement descending
    viii.   Descending then ascending, root movement descending

Full-range scales, lowest scale tone to highest scale tone

    i.   All ascending, root movement ascending
    ii.   All descending, root movement ascending
    iii.   Ascending then descending, root movement ascending
    iv.   Descending then ascending, root movement ascending
    v.   All ascending, root movement descending
    vi.   All descending, root movement descending
    vii.   Ascending then descending, root movement descending
    viii.   Descending then ascending, root movement descending

Major Third Root Movement

Repeat the exercises again, this time using major third root movement. You will now have four sets per exercise, for example:

    Set one: E—G♯/A♭—C
    Set two: F—A—C♯/D♭
    Set three: F♯/G♭—A♯/B♭—D
    Set four: G—B—D♯/E♭

The exercises again:

Single-octave scales

    i.   All ascending, low to high
    ii.   All ascending, high to low
    iii.   All descending, low to high
    iv.   All descending, high to low

v. Ascending then descending, low to high
vi. Ascending then descending, high to low
vii. Descending then ascending, low to high
viii. Descending then ascending, high to low

Two-octave scales
i. All ascending, low to high
ii. All ascending, high to low
iii. All descending, low to high
iv. All descending, high to low
v. Ascending then descending, low to high
vi. Ascending then descending, high to low
vii. Descending then ascending, low to high
viii. Descending then ascending, high to low

Three-octave scales
i. All ascending, low to high
ii. All ascending, high to low
iii. All descending, low to high
iv. All descending, high to low
v. Ascending then descending, low to high
vi. Ascending then descending, high to low
vii. Descending then ascending, low to high
viii. Descending then ascending, high to low

Full-range scales, lowest root to highest root
i. All ascending, root movement ascending
ii. All descending, root movement ascending
iii. Ascending then descending, root movement ascending
iv. Descending then ascending, root movement ascending
v. All ascending, root movement descending
vi. All descending, root movement descending
vii. Ascending then descending, root movement descending
viii. Descending then ascending, root movement descending

Full-range scales, lowest scale tone to highest scale tone
i. All ascending, root movement ascending
ii. All descending, root movement ascending
iii. Ascending then descending, root movement ascending
iv. Descending then ascending, root movement ascending
v. All ascending, root movement descending
vi. All descending, root movement descending
vii. Ascending then descending, root movement descending
viii. Descending then ascending, root movement descending

Perfect Fourth Root Movement

Once you reach root movements larger than major thirds, things get a bit tricky. You can't just apply the exercises in the same way because by doing so with perfect fourths you'll either quickly run out of range on almost all instruments, or you'll technically have to practice a mix of perfect fourth root movement and their inversion—perfect fifth root movement—so as to maintain the structure of the exercise. For example: if you're practicing ascending one-octave scales on guitar with perfect fourth root movement, you'll be fine from E to A to D, but in order to practice the lowest octave of the G scale you'd have to drop down a fifth rather than ascend a fourth. So not all of these exercises will be great fits for every instrument; nonetheless, they are definitely worth working through. With that in mind, here are some rules to keep in mind so as to maximize the effectiveness of each exercise and minimize the number of walls you'll hit:

–   Never jump a scale root more than an octave—we want to hit as many adjacent scales as possible.
–   Only make jumps on the first note of the scale, never in the middle of a scale.
–   Only make a jump when you're running out of range.
–   Try to practice each scale in each octave possible on your instrument; in other words, if your instrument can play the G scale in three octaves, make sure to hit each octave in each exercise if possible.

The exercises:

Single-octave scales
     i.   All ascending, low to high
     ii.   All ascending, high to low
     iii. All descending, low to high
     iv. All descending, high to low
     v.   Ascending then descending, low to high
     vi. Ascending then descending, high to low
     vii. Descending then ascending, low to high
     viii. Descending then ascending, high to low

Two-octave scales
     i.   All ascending, low to high
     ii.   All ascending, high to low
     iii. All descending, low to high
     iv. All descending, high to low
     v.   Ascending then descending, low to high
     vi. Ascending then descending, high to low
     vii. Descending then ascending, low to high
     viii. Descending then ascending, high to low

Three-octave scales
     i.   All ascending, low to high
     ii.   All ascending, high to low
     iii. All descending, low to high
     iv. All descending, high to low
     v.   Ascending then descending, low to high
     vi. Ascending then descending, high to low
     vii. Descending then ascending, low to high
     viii. Descending then ascending, high to low

Full-range scales, lowest root to highest root
     i.   All ascending, root movement ascending
     ii.   All descending, root movement ascending
     iii. Ascending then descending, root movement ascending
     iv. Descending then ascending, root movement ascending
     v.   All ascending, root movement descending
     vi. All descending, root movement descending
     vii. Ascending then descending, root movement descending
     viii. Descending then ascending, root movement descending

Full-range scales, lowest scale tone to highest scale tone

i. All ascending, root movement ascending
ii. All descending, root movement ascending
iii. Ascending then descending, root movement ascending
iv. Descending then ascending, root movement ascending
v. All ascending, root movement descending
vi. All descending, root movement descending
vii. Ascending then descending, root movement descending
viii. Descending then ascending, root movement descending

Tritone Root Movement

This is the last section of different root movement exercises. Intervals larger than tritones are inversions of smaller intervals; for example, a perfect fifth is an inversion of a perfect fourth, as discussed in the perfect fourth section. As such, practicing perfect fifth root movement with the various directional movements has already been covered when practicing perfect fourth root movement. The biggest hassle with practicing tritone root movements is that you have to do each exercise six times: a tritone inverts to itself (for example, the tritone of C is F♯/G♭; if you're practicing single-octave scales, all ascending from low to high, you would play C major, for example, then G♭ major; then you'd have to do another pair, let's say C♯/D♭ major, and it's tritone: G. As such, you'd end up with six pairs: C—F♯/G♭; C♯/D♭—G; D—G♯/A♭; D♯/E♭—A; E—A♯/B♭; F—B).

Again, the exercises:

Single-octave scales

i. All ascending, low to high
ii. All ascending, high to low
iii. All descending, low to high
iv. All descending, high to low
v. Ascending then descending, low to high
vi. Ascending then descending, high to low
vii. Descending then ascending, low to high
viii. Descending then ascending, high to low

Two-octave scales

i. All ascending, low to high
ii. All ascending, high to low
iii. All descending, low to high
iv. All descending, high to low
v. Ascending then descending, low to high
vi. Ascending then descending, high to low
vii. Descending then ascending, low to high
viii. Descending then ascending, high to low

Three-octave scales

i. All ascending, low to high
ii. All ascending, high to low
iii. All descending, low to high
iv. All descending, high to low
v. Ascending then descending, low to high
vi. Ascending then descending, high to low
vii. Descending then ascending, low to high
viii. Descending then ascending, high to low

Full-range scales, lowest root to highest root

    i.   All ascending, root movement ascending
    ii.   All descending, root movement ascending
    iii.   Ascending then descending, root movement ascending
    iv.   Descending then ascending, root movement ascending
    v.   All ascending, root movement descending
    vi.   All descending, root movement descending
    vii.   Ascending then descending, root movement descending
    viii. Descending then ascending, root movement descending

Full-range scales, lowest scale tone to highest scale tone

    i.   All ascending, root movement ascending
    ii.   All descending, root movement ascending
    iii.   Ascending then descending, root movement ascending
    iv.   Descending then ascending, root movement ascending
    v.   All ascending, root movement descending
    vi.   All descending, root movement descending
    vii.   Ascending then descending, root movement descending
    viii. Descending then ascending, root movement descending

Part Two

This section explores the various intervallic ways in which to play a single scale. The methodology is similar to the first section and in fact can be applied to the first section to exponentially increase the number of exercises to practice. More on that later; this section explores ways to practice scales in thirds, fourths, fifths, sixths, and sevenths. Larger intervals such as ninths and 11^{ths} can be practiced in the same way, but aren't demonstrated. Likewise, each interval is practiced in pairs, groups of three, and groups of four, but there is no reason why one couldn't practice in larger note groupings like five or seven.

Since the exercises below focus on ways to practice a single individual scale (be it any single individual scale or mode), all examples will be written in C Major for the sake of clarity.

Single-octave scales in thirds

Pairs

All ascending, low to high

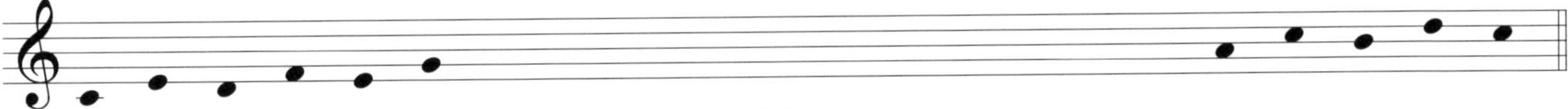

All ascending, high to low

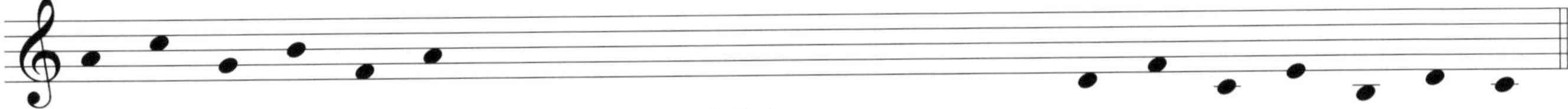

All descending, low to high

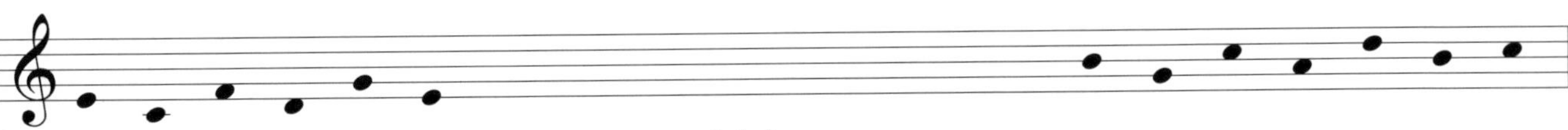

All descending, high to low

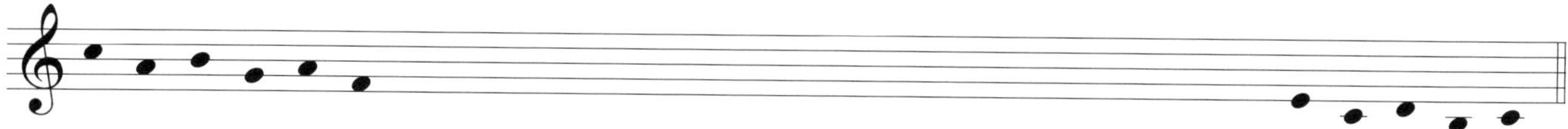

Ascending then descending, low to high

Ascending then descending, high to low

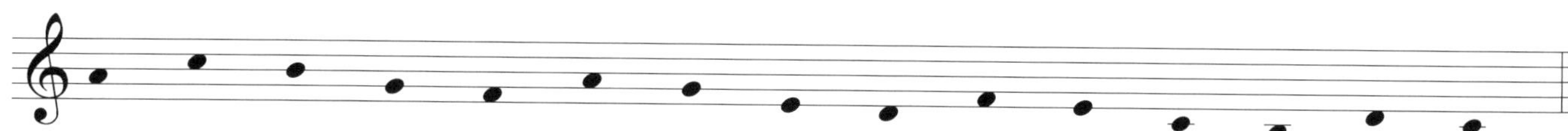

Descending then ascending, low to high

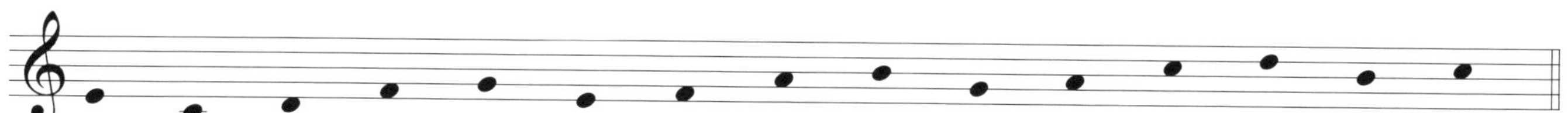

Descending then ascending, high to low

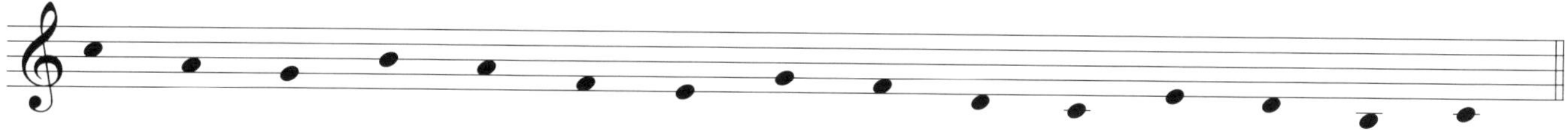

Groups of three

All ascending, low to high

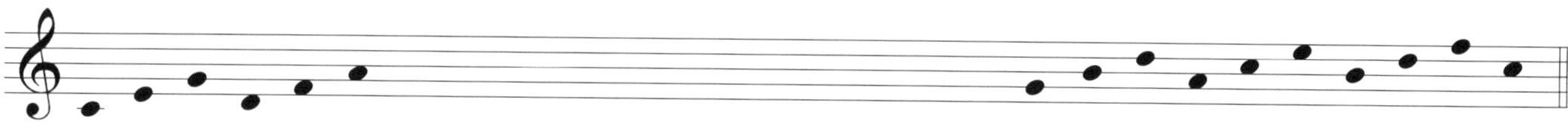

All ascending, high to low

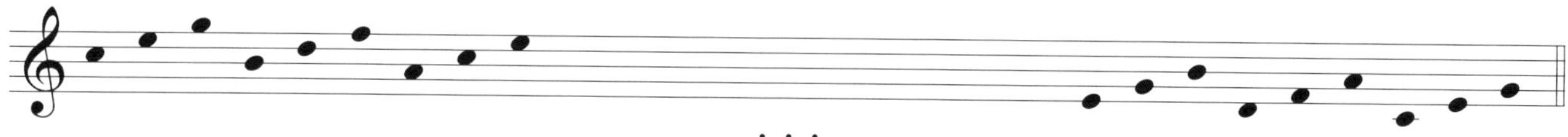

All descending, low to high

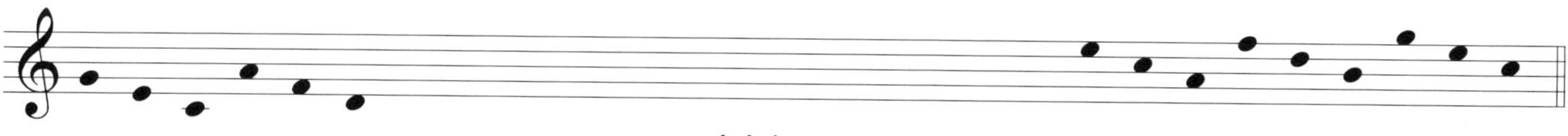

All descending, high to low

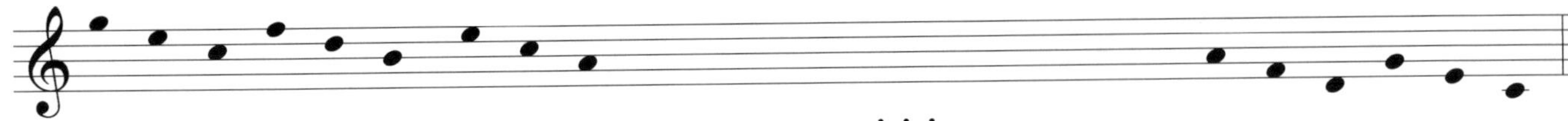

Ascending then descending, low to high

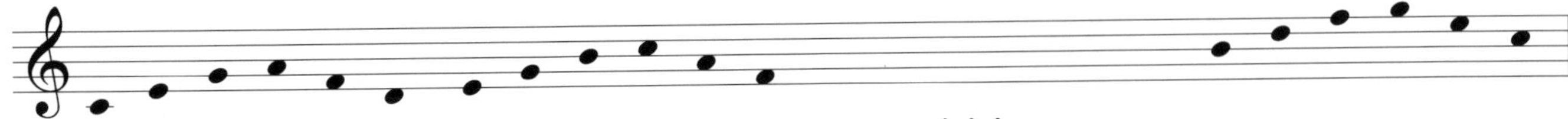

Ascending then descending, high to low

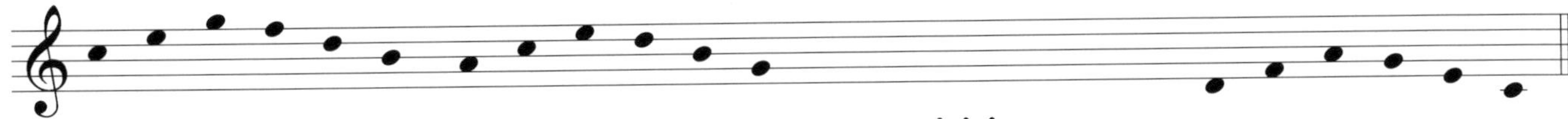

Descending then ascending, low to high

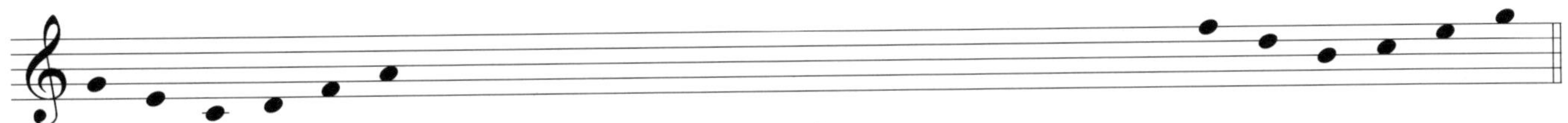

Descending then ascending, high to low

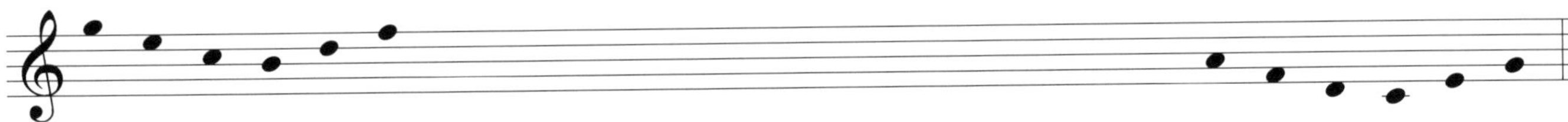

Groups of four

All ascending, low to high

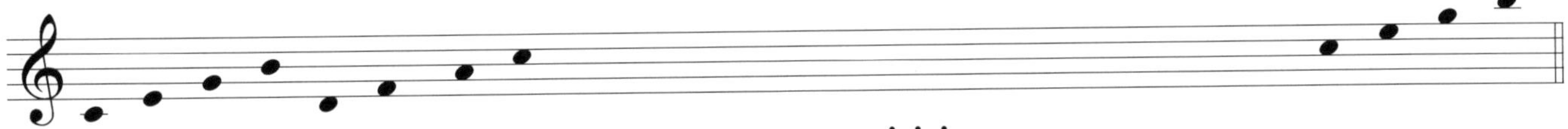

All ascending, high to low

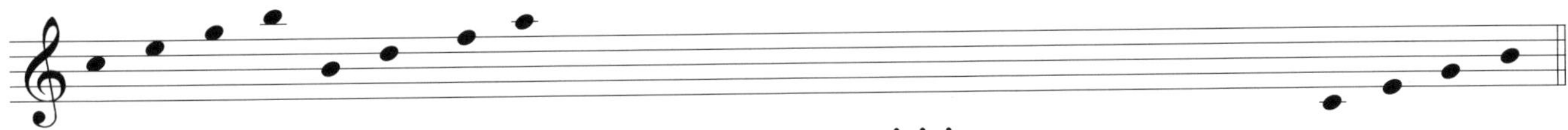

All descending, low to high

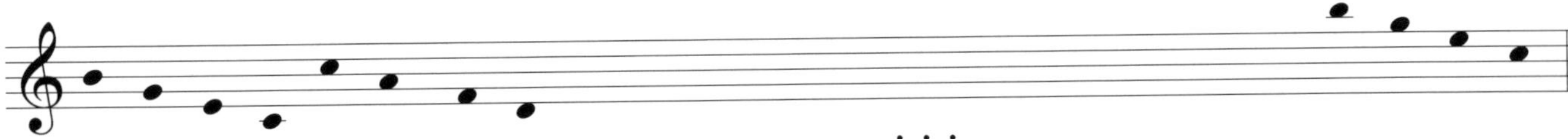

All descending, high to low

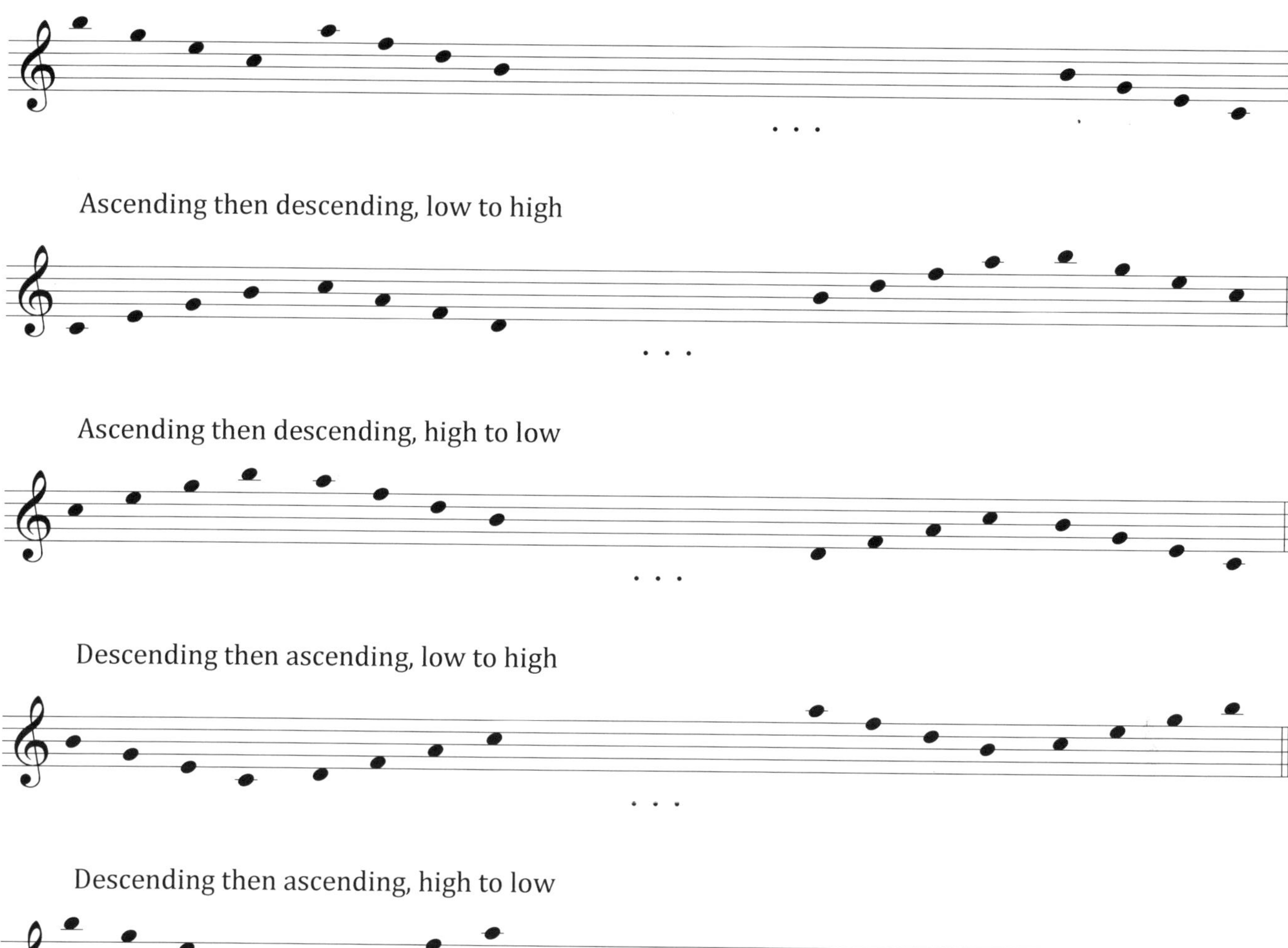

Ascending then descending, low to high

Ascending then descending, high to low

Descending then ascending, low to high

Descending then ascending, high to low

After completing the exercises for single-octave scales in thirds, repeat them for two-octave scales in thirds, then three-octave scales in thirds, then full-range scales in thirds (lowest root to highest root), then full range scales in thirds (lowest scale tone to highest scale tone). Then, practice the exercises again using fourths rather than thirds. Once you complete practicing fourths, move on to fifths, sixths, and finally intervals of sevenths. Again, you can practice larger intervals as well using the same methodology, or larger groupings than four-note groups.

Finally: there is no reason one can't take a specific intervallic way of practicing a scale and run it through section one of the book. For example, you could practice a major scale in fourths, using three note groups. That could be run through the various chromatic root movement exercises, then whole-step root movement exercises, and so on. It is worth mentioning that you will drive yourself crazy if you try to practice every single variation of every single possible exercise presented in this book or potentially derived from this book. I urge you to remember the goals of this book: a) master your instrument; b) increase tactile familiarity; c) improve facility; d) improve velocity; e) improve tone; f) improve technique. Each of those goals can be attained without necessarily going through every single possible iteration of everything. So have fun, don't practice through pain, and know that there are ultimately more important and interesting things in music and in life than practicing scales!

Part Three

If by now you don't share my sentiment of loathing practicing scales, you may have some sort of severe issue. Nonetheless, I have several additional levels of scalar torture for you, albeit in suggestion only:

I.   Return to section one. Rather than simply practicing a single scale, pair two scales… or three or four. You may, for example, pair a major scale with a super locrian mode.

II. Perhaps use different intervallic groupings. Going with the example above, consider practicing a major scale in fourths with a super locrian scale in thirds.

III. Use different note and rhythmic groupings. You could practice a major scale in fourths, in three-note groupings, with a super locrian scale in thirds, in four-note groupings. As such, you could experiment with maintaining note value versus making a group of four constitute sixteenth notes and a group of three constitute triplets.

End Note

You can be a master of your instrument; you can be a master of rhythm, harmony, timbre, dynamics, and every other element of music; but if you don't express yourself, you're probably going to be playing some pretty meaningless music. The music I personally love the most is innovative, is performed (relatively) flawlessly by master instrumentalists (including vocalists), and most importantly *says something*. There is music that is indeed technically masterful that just doesn't move me; there is also music that I cannot justify liking, save for the fact it just moves me. This book will absolutely help you conquer your instrument and improve your theoretical knowledge. But we need more awesome music, and to do that you need to set this book down and go experience life. I firmly believe that the best music is yet to come, and I hope this book has had some impact to that end.

Thanks so much for your support—if you found this useful, please check out my other books—and then go outside, or put on your favorite album, or adopt a rescue dog, or do anything that isn't practicing scales!

About the Author

Collin Bay began studying music as a four-year-old. He attended Interlochen Arts Academy and was part of the Interlochen Jazz Octet, recipient of Downbeat Magazine's top student award. He studied with Vijay Iyer and John Scofield at New School University in New York City. Fluent on many instruments and in many styles, he has performed on four continents both as a solo artist and as a member of various ensembles. He has shared the stage with MacArthur Fellows and has appeared on albums that have cracked the top-20 on iTunes world music chart. Having begun at Mel Bay editing books as a teen, Collin now works in Artist Relations and Product Development for the company. He resides in St. Louis and enjoys running with his dog. He is Mel Bay's youngest grandson.

WWW.MELBAY.COM

Made in the USA
Monee, IL
07 July 2026

56551283R00015